Real Estate Investing for Passive Income

A practical guide to succeed in your business thanks to marketing strategies and crisis management tips

Neal Hooper

TABLE OF CONTENTS

Marketing & Sales Plan

Marketing your house to sell is an invaluable process. You already know the faster you can sell the property, the quicker you will recoup your investment and make a profit. The housing market can be a competitive one, so it is essential to market your house across multiple channels virtually. Marketing includes both online and offline activities. You don't need to have a marketing experience to market your house effectively, but you need to understand what works and what doesn't.

Strategies That Work

When considering your different marketing options, you want to focus on practical strategies while also being cost-efficient. When deciding how to market the house, talk to your realtor first, if you are working with one. Your realtor should undoubtedly help tremendously with this part, as it is also in his best interest to sell the house quickly. There are three options in offline marketing that you should consider: print advertising, yard signs, and networking.

Print Advertising

It includes advertising in local papers and house sale magazines. This type of advertising can be costly, depending on the area you are living in. However, if you are planning a large open house, you may want to take the chance. A lot of people still check the newspaper when looking for local open houses. Print advertising is also a great way to get your name out there. It is helpful if you build your flipping business and have houses to sell regularly.

Yard Signs

Yard signs have proven to be very useful. For numerous people discerning buying a house, it is not uncommon to drive around the neighborhoods where they want to live searching for "For Sale" signs. Sometimes people aren't necessarily looking to buy a house, but merely driving through a neighborhood, they like and see a "For Sale" sign. Yard signs also encourage word-of- mouth marketing. Neighbors are more likely to tell people they know are looking to buy a house. Yard signs can be purchased for a relatively low price at a hardware store or through a printing company. You can even order generic "For Sale" posters featuring your company name and contact information so that the same sign can be used over and over again. If you have the help of a real estate agent, they likely already have signs that can be used at your property, so this will be a no expense.

Networking

Another essential form of marketing that people often overlook is networking. Let people know you have a house for sale. Offer a referral fee to anyone who finds you a legitimate buyer. See if there are any professional organizations in your area that cater to landlords or other property investors. For example, in Lorain County, Ohio, an organization called the Lake Erie Landlord Association. They have monthly meetings, and part of their monthly meeting is what they call "Buy, Sell, and Trade." It is when members can stand up and make announcements regarding the properties they have for sale. Other members may be interested in buying the house, or they can help spread the word. These types of organizations can be crucial to your long-term success as a house flipper.

Creating Your Website

Even though you're starting with just one property, you want to be prepared for your business to overgrow. Creating a website now will enable you to start building your online presence so that when you have houses for sale, you are already established online. Additionally, you can advertise other companies through your website and make your website independently profitable as part of your overall business

Internet Marketing

Internet marketing has become a significant source of marketing for real estate.

Many buyers, particularly young buyers, are looking online before contacting realtors or sellers. They want to gather as much information as they can to make an informed decision more quickly.

For that reason, you must have an online marketing strategy, and you make sure all the vital information regarding the properties you have for sale is easily accessible online.

Content Marketing

Content marketing refers to the marketing of content you create and post online. It can include written content, images, and videos. Content marketing, if done correctly, can be highly effective. The one downside to marketing a house online yourself is that the big realty companies already have a significant amount of clout online regarding search engine rankings, so you will need to work harder to be seen.

The first method that you need to do is write a detailed description of the property. Write a description of each room and a significant feature in the house. You want to use many descriptive words to make the house sound as amazingly inviting and desirable as possible. You then need to take your written description, the images you took and edited for marketing purposes, and the video you created and post them online in as many different places as possible.

Writing Sales Copy

Writing sales copy is an industry of its own. It is a way of writing that makes the product appeal to consumers on a psychological level. Copywriters are well trained in using descriptive words and phrases to get an emotional reaction out of readers. While you can't learn how to be an effective copywriter overnight, you can pursue ways to improve your descriptions' quality.

To do this, you can hire a copywriter to write your descriptions for you. You can learn basic copywriting and do it yourself, or you can hire a copywriter who is willing to work with you to help you improve your descriptions. The route you choose will depend on how much time and money you want to invest in getting this done. It is one example of when it might be best to preserve your time for more critical tasks and hiring someone to write the descriptions for you.

Social Media Marketing

Social media marketing is another useful branch of online marketing. To market your house through social media, you need to strategically post the descriptions, images, and videos you created to multiple social networks and web pages. For example, search Facebook for any local pages that allow people to post things they have for sale. It would be best if you did the same with Twitter and Google+. Post images of the house on Instagram and Pinterest. Post the video of your house on YouTube.

With every social network posting, you should include links back to your website or the base website where your sales information is posted. In addition to having relations back to your website, you should include contact information with every posting. You can't assume people will follow your links.

Encourage your acquaintances and family to like and share your posts. Although they may not be personally interested, every time they like or share the post, all of their social contacts will see the post. The more the data is shared, the better your chances will be to reach the people looking to buy.

Virtual Staging

Another thing you can do is offer virtual staging. There are a couple of ways you can go about this. First, you can stage the house before taking pictures, so when people look online, it will be what they see if they visit the place. Another thing you can do is create an interactive floor plan. It will allow users to see how furniture can be arranged in space.

If they have the measurements for their furniture, they can make sure it will fit in various rooms and through the doorway or stairs. Virtual staging can increase the likelihood that searchers will visit the actual house.

Creating Marketing Material

If you don't have any help with a realtor, you will need to make your marketing material. Even if you are working with a realtor, you may want to create marketing material to ensure it is done to your standards. It requires only a brief search online to find humorous marketing failures committed by realtors.

Additionally, understanding the type of marketing materials you need and the standard you want them to be will help you know quickly if the realtor is not doing a great job.

- Fliers

- Photos

- Video

- Selling Binders

- Business Card

Open Houses and Showings

Open houses and showings are opportunities for potential buyers to tour the house, ask questions, and decide if they are interested.

The open house is like the big production you've been carefully planning for.

You want the place to look its best, and you want the open house to be well-advertised, so many people show up. Having a large number of people come to the open house will increase your networking opportunities and word-of-mouth advertising, and it will promote the place in the minds of those that attend.

They will see how many other people appear to be interested in the house, increasing the pressure to make an offer quickly.

Developing A Practical Strategy

With so many marketing strategies at your disposal, it is best to create a practical marketing strategy that you will follow utilizing both online and offline marketing tactics. Creating an actual plan will ensure that everything is done effectively and appropriately.

Going into a marketing campaign without a plan will result in missed and overall stress and frustration.

The easiest way to make sure everything is completed and without stress is to plan everything out in advance.

It is not a situation where "winging it" will be sufficient.

It is important to remember you own the house; it costs you money. The goal is to sell it and sell it fast.

Creating A Marketing Calendar

A significant part of your marketing strategy will be creating a marketing calendar. It will include the dates that ads will be in the newspaper and published online. It will also have the deadlines for newspapers and other outlets to ensure the information is published on the days you want it to be public.

Your calendar should consist of when and where you will be getting the fliers printed and yard signs prepared. Every marketing activity you partake in should be scheduled, so you don't miss deadlines.

The Exit Strategy: Finding Buyers

Finding buyers isn't difficult at all. Selling is the fun part because that's when you'll see the money you've worked hard for. You'll be offering a much needed, valued service. Think about the people who will most likely be leasing from you. They were maybe getting out of foreclosure or bankruptcy. After having a house, it's tough to squeeze the two kids, the dog, and puss into an apartment again. Back then, it was just himself and his wife; now he's got a family and all that stuff in the garage. This person needs a home like yours to put up his family; their credit is not so good right now due to some problems.

When I qualify my buyers, I don't focus that much on credit, only to the point of qualifying them eventually, say in 1-2 years. It works out just fine since I'll need that time anyway to make sure the property appraises a higher amount than when I took it over.

It's best to use a loan officer to prequalify your buyers. This way, they will stay with your buyers and help them qualify to be a loan for them at the end of the lease term.

What happens if the buyers don't qualify or are not ready by the end of the term? Then renew the lease with the option and increase the lease amount, and the price of the property also goes up, not by much but say an extra $10,000. It's time to move into your exit and back end strategy.

Your exit strategies could be:

Leasing – You could do a straight rental and rent forever.
Selling – You could turn around a sell to an end buyer.

Lease with Option – My favorite exit strategy because you're helping someone who might have problems buying immediately, so you're giving them a chance to own.

Deciding the Exit Strategy

It depends on what you've got because you can only sell what you've got. For example, if you acquired the property with no equity, then it wouldn't make sense to turn around and sell right away. It means you'll have to Sell High and Sell Long, meaning sell it in 2-3 years instead of now or a year from now. Likewise, if you acquired the property and you used my bank negotiation strategy to create equity and reduce the principal balance, then you could afford to Sell Low. Meaning you can wholesale or sell just below full value and make a quick profit without touching or repairing it.

The fact is, there are buyers everywhere who will be waiting in line to get into your houses. I have more buyers than I have houses for. I have a small business in Florida who will pay me top dollar to house their employees; I have people relocating to Los Angeles who need a home, they call me up begging me to find them a place that they can rent to own, and the list goes on and on. If you didn't already guess, you could do business in all the states you want, so if it's not working for you where you are, then take it somewhere else. I like to take the show on the road, and even though I'm living in Los Angeles, I'm able to put under contract and take over properties in New York and Florida. How would you like to do that?

Filling Your Homes Super-Fast

Advertising for buyers continuously is the way you keep your homes leased. The best way to start this business is to find your buyer first. Advertise for your buyer first so that you can see who's in your market and what they want. I've always liked the rent to own concept. It's a popular way to sell used cars, furniture, and even appliances in most cities. By far, the best rent to own application is in real estate, which we call the lease/option deal. It is my favorite part of the transaction when I put a deserving family into my homes. When you offer a rent to own home, you provide excellent service, and people will pay premium rent for this opportunity. If you keep this in mind, it will help you to structure your deals going in.

Rent To Own – No Bank Qualifying

Beautiful three bedroom/ 2 bath home, close to all, rent with the option to buy 1 or 2 years. Credit problems OK, your job is your credit.

You get paid three ways:

• Get paid by a non-refundable deposit called an option fee. This fee is a consideration that the buyer pays you to option your home.

• Get paid on the spread between the mortgage payment and the money you receive monthly from your buyer, who is also leasing from you.

• Get paid from the profit you make at the end of the transaction when the buyer exercises his option to buy and gets a mortgage and cashes you out. It's the difference between what you paid and the price at which you sell the house.

•   Get paid from the tax deduction from depreciation, property expense deductions, and mortgage interest deductions.

Processing Your Tenant-Buyers

Does it just like a management company because that's what you are now? If you don't like this part of the

business, you can hire a property manager or use a Realtor® to lease up the home.

Negotiating The Sale To Maximize Your Profit

Differentiating Seemingly Similar Offers

When regular homeowners sell their possessions, they often act as auctioneers looking for the high bid, but the worth is only one constituent of an offer (or

purchase arrangement).

In numerous cases, a lower offer is more significant if the buyer can close quickly and doesn't demand many accompaniments, such as closing charges and repairs.

When you're flipping properties, you need to be able to evaluate offers and see beyond price to weigh all factors.

Discuss with your agent for detailed guidance on matters that concern you.

Does the buyer have a stable fund?

A buyer doesn't need to be able to pay for your house to bid on it. He can have a dollar in his wallet and ten dollars in his savings account and still submit an offer.

If you accept the offer by signing the purchase agreement, he can tie up your property for several days of discussions until you notice that he can't get supporting fund.

When gathering offers, don't sign a purchase contract unless the buyer provides proof of one of the following financing types:

Cash: Cash offers are the best, but you should confirm that the bidder has the existing cash to close the transaction. Authentication can be in the arrangement of a letter from the bidder's bank or credit union or from Grandma Rowland, who's putting up the money. You can also ask for a copy of the buyers' recent bank statements — advise the buyers to blackout their account numbers to not fall into the wrong hands. Suppose you can't get the actual statements, or the buyers prefer not to provide copies of bank statements. In that case, the bank can provide an official letter stating sufficient funds are available in the buyers' accounts.

Preapproval: Preapproval means that a moneylender has already approved the loan. This offer is the subsequently best thing to a cash offer, but preapproval letters are worth only as much as the paper they're published on. Ask the bidders to talk with your mortgage person (a loan officer you trust or one your agent recommends). Don't trust the buyer's loan officer's word because that person may not be the most dependable source of precise data. If the bidders hesitate at this proposal, tell them that buying and financing a home is an important business. They wouldn't have significant operation without getting a subsequent opinion, so they should consider getting some additional input from your loan officer. More than likely, your mortgage professional will be of a higher caliber than the one that are helping them.

Pre-qualification: If the buyer has pre-qualification, a moneylender has investigated the bidder's financial accounts and decided that the buyer can probably esure a loan. Pre- qualification is one rung down from preapproval.

All things being equal, a cash offer is best, but if the cash offer is more than 5 % lower than a noncash offer, you have to weigh the benefits against the lower purchase price.

How "earnest" is the buyer?

Most offers have an earnest-money deposit attached to them that shows how committed the buyer is to purchase the property. If the bidder hesistates out of the transaction without due cause, he forfeits the earnest money deposit, and you get to keep it. An offer with a sizeable earnest-money deposit is less likely to fall apart at the last minute than an offer with a smaller deposit. To the seller, having that assurance carries a lot of weight.

What else is the buyer requesting for?

Bidders ask for all sorts of matter when they submit a proposal. They may ask you to eradicate that pool you just installed, thinking it would boost the house's value. They can inquire for the sports car you have parked in your garage. They can demand that you pay up to 6 % of their closing charges, pay for a home warranty, or immediately vacate the property at closing. When evaluating an offer, consider all these requests. The succeeding are propositions on how to manage common appeals:

Possession at closing. Buyers often want to take instant ownership of a property. When you're flipping, this condition is perfect, assuming you don't reside in the property. If you're living in the property you flip, come up a contingency plan, and attempt to do your best to put up this request.

It may troublesome to you, but as a flipper, you want to sell your house as fast as possible to cut your holding expenses and have the cash to fund your subsequent flip.

Payment of closing costs. Many first-time homeowners request that the seller pays a portion of the closing costs, so they don't have to pay these charges upfront. If buyers ask for closing charges, consider proposing to pay the closing expenses upfront if they are keen to pay a little more for the house to cover the closing expenses. Many first-time buyers would instead roll the closing costs into their mortgage than pay the fees upfront. Of course, this is only a choice if the property appraises the amount the buyers are willing to pay. If the appraisal comes in too low, you can challenge it, but you need to lower the price if you lose that battle.

No tax proration. At closing, you usually get back any taxes you paid for the months that the new owner will live in the property. When buyers demand to no tax proration, they're demanding you to pay their property taxes. Ask your title company to compute the amount you would be receiving back at closing. If the sum is small — only a few hundred bucks — you may want to settle to this request. If you just paid the tax bill and the sale closes in the first month after paying, that money should be reimbursed to you. For example, if the taxes are $3,000 for the year, which equals

$250 a month, you lose $2,750 at closing if you give up tax proration.

What conditions has the buyer included?

Conditional statements (weasel clauses) go together with every offer. Some are made into the proposal, but the buyer can jot down different conditions. If you're smart, you probably did the same thing when you bought the house. The succeeding are the most common circumstances buyers demand:

Financing must be approved. Every purchase agreement has this condition, and if you're already screening out anyone who's not prequalified for a loan, this clause shouldn't pose a problem.

The property must appraise at the sale price or higher. If you've completed your lesson and priced your property competitively, this situation shouldn't pose a problem.

The property must pass the inspection. You had the property inspected when you bought it, and you renovated everything, so this point is another nonissue. The title must be pure. Before you acquired the house, you investigated the title and acquired title insurance, so you're safe here, too. My existing home must sell first. You don't want the sale of your house hanging in limbo because the buyers can't sell their house. If you like the offer, consider countering with an offer that gives the prospective buyers first right of refusal, which keeps the house on the market but provides the buyers with notice (often 72 hours) before you sell to someone else. The buyers then have that much time (72 hours, for example) to match any offer you obtain. If you don't like the proposal, give your other offers a higher priority.

How soon does the buyer demand to close?

As a flipper, you're well mindful of holding expenses. Every day, your property costs you money, so the faster you close, the less money you expend. When differentiating proposals, check the date on which the buyer desires to close. If one buyer who desires to close immediately offers $2,000 less than another buyer who wants to close a month from now, the lower offer may be the better offer, assuming all other conditions are equal.

Mastering the Art Of Counteroffers

Some offers are so low that all you can do is laugh and shrug them off, but no offer is too low to reject outright in most cases. When you obtain an offer that seems to be a little irrational, don't take it personally. If you're not prepared to say either "yes" or "no," reply with your counteroffer.

Submitting a counteroffer

After you obtain and assess a reasonable proposal, you have two choices — you can agree to take the offer as is or submit a counteroffer in letter. If the buyer proposed the full price and attractive terms, agree to take the proposal immediately. Don't start to second-guess yourself or think whether you sold yourself short. Lady Fortune has smiled down upon you, so smile back and sign the agreement.

If the proposal isn't stellar but shows some potential for negotiation, craft a counteroffer.

Coming up with a savvy counteroffer

Offering and counteroffering is like a chess game, in which buyer and seller attempt to anticipate one another's succeeding move. You never can never tell what a buyer is going to demand or state as a condition, so you need to tread cautiously and think creatively

Putting your counteroffer in a letter

If you decide to counter, write your counteroffer on the copy of the purchase agreement you received from the buyer or the buyer's agent, initial your changes, and either fax or hand- deliver your counteroffer to the buyer's agent or directly to the buyer if she's not working through an agent. (Some agents prefer to submit counteroffers on a separate form instead of marking up the original offer; they number the counteroffers something along the lines of Seller 1, Buyer 2, Seller 3, and so on.) If you're using an agent, have your agent present the counteroffer. Be sure to stipulate the time in which the buyer needs to respond to your counteroffer.

Leveraging the power of multiple offers

When you receive an outstanding offer, jump on it. If the offer falls short of outstanding, call your other prospects and let them know that you've received an offer and are going to pursue it if you don't receive an offer from them by a particular deadline (one or two days). This tactic applies pressure to all interested parties, encouraging them to get off their duffs and act quickly or lose the house for good. Keep the details about the offer you received a mystery, so new bidders don't have an unfair advantage.

If additional offers arrive, you can now compare offers and accept the best offer or counter it. However, keep a copy of those other offers on hand just if what you consider to be the best offer falls through.

Prepping for closing

To ensure that the closing proceeds as smoothly as possible, supply your closing agent with any documents she may need to put together the closing packets. Documents typically include the following:

Termite inspection report. If the buyer is financing the purchase with a Veterans Affairs (VA) loan, immediately schedule a termite inspection, if it hasn't already been done, and send the report to the closing agent or attorney handling the closing. (Typically, the buyer orders the termite inspection and has it done before closing, and the seller pays for it at closing.)

Purchase agreement and any appendices.

Mortgage payoff information and any second mortgages or other liens.

Buyer's financial information.

Closing The Deal

"You have yourself a deal."

If you ask us, there are no better words in business. You will never forget your first deal. For some people, it takes a few weeks; for some, it takes months. It took Alex Saenz nine months to close his first deal, and he credits all of his success in battling through those difficult times.

Whenever you finally close your first deal, none of the tough times matter and a euphoric relief will race over you. For many people, their first check is likely the biggest payday of your life. Now it's time to get your buyers together, take the deal to the title company, and get paid. You have done all of the hard work; now it's time to finish the process.

Finding a Title Agency

Working with a great title agency will make you a fortune and save you headaches along the way. Not every title company understands wholesaling, though, and the last thing you want is to have a deal fall through at the end because you chose the wrong title agency. Finding an investor-friendly title agency isn't tricky, but it is essential. The right title agency will ensure everything runs smoothly while also saving you money on fees (they will usually give you a 20-30% discount if you find the right title agency).

The best way to find a title agency is by referral. Your networking from Facebook Groups and REIA's should make finding a title agency simple. Getting referred is the best way to find a great partner to help things run smoothly. If you are struggling to find a referral, Google "title agencies" and start making phone calls to find an "investor-friendly title agency that works with wholesalers." That jargon should tell them all they need to know.

Pre-Qualify Your Buyers

You know what the house is worth, you know what repair costs are (estimated), and you know the price you need to receive to satisfy your fee. It's time to send pictures and numbers to your buyers' list to see who is interested. Make sure to send the full set of photos so buyers can see the whole picture. There is no point in trying to "trick" buyers into thinking a situation is better than it is. If you attempt to mislead a buyer, they will find out once they view the property, and you risk wasting everyone's time. They should be able to see the photos and your asking price. Make sure to include your fee and feel free to start a little higher than your bottom line. If you have a massive buyers list, you can be more selective, but many buyers will try to negotiate down. If you start with a higher number, the worst- case scenario is they accept it, and you make a higher profit.

Walking Buyers Through Properties

The more comfortable you can make this on the seller, the better. You don't want to scare the seller because you bring in ten people over a week to view the house. Try to narrow it down to a handful and tell the seller that these are your partners, contractors, or financial partners. Do NOT tell them that this is the end buyer.

After the buyers walk through the property, they will present you with a firm offer, and you can select which works best for you. The goal is to do with the buyer that gives the highest offer, as long as everything else is equal.

For example, one buyer may make an offer that is $5000 higher, but if they take 30-days to close, you may be better working with the buyer to close within 7-10 days.

The name of the game is getting paid and working towards your next deal.

Assigning the Contract

Once you have confirmed the offer and the deal is done, it's time to open escrow and get to the title agency. Again, make sure that your buyer can close in no more than 14 days, but hopefully less than 10.

When you get to the title agency, the end buyer will open up the escrow, and to make sure they are serious buyers, request that they put down at least $5000 to start that process. As soon as the escrow process begins, all mortgages, liens, or debts will be paid first. It is essential to ask in the buying process because all debts should be built into your offer to the seller. There is nothing worse than losing a deal because you didn't know they still owe money on the home.

If you are wondering which contract you should use, we will send you the same agreement we have used to close over 1500 deals.

Getting Paid

As soon as all debts are paid off, the seller gets paid, you get your fee, and the buyer receives the deed to the house. The seller walks away free and clear, with cash in their pocket. You walk away with your check for all of your hard work, and the seller will gain a valuable asset. The title agency will handle the entire transaction, and they will disperse funds via check or bank account wire.

Neal Hooper

Postgame Analysis

Since you've sold your property, it's an excellent opportunity to make a stride back and investigate your arrangement. It's essential to do this toward the finish of

every real estate exchange to make sense of what you did well and what you fouled up. It's dependably a smart thought to contrast your anticipated with your genuine benefit and perceive where things worked and where they didn't. It will shield you from committing a similar error twice.

To be fantastic or uncommon at any control, you need to move in the direction of acing your specialty reliably. If we work, work, work relentlessly while never taking one moment to dissect what we're doing, we'll never distinguish where we have to improve. By ceasing to audit what we're doing and where we are going, we keep on recognizing enhancements and efficiencies that will quicken our business. Above all, the time you take to survey a past arrangement will enable you to get more cash-flow on a future arrangement. Working without really breaking down on the off chance that we are, truth be told, improving keeps us from showing signs of improvement and heading the correct way. It is significant that we, as a whole, set aside the effort to investigate and postgame our endeavors and gain from our great and terrible application. When we postgame appropriately, we can enhance each extends we complete.

Each rehabber ought to do what I call a postgame examination after each project. It will help you determine whether you effectively assessed rehab costs, holding times and whether you made an enormous enough benefit. Frameworks are essential to your prosperity and won't be as powerful without legitimate principles. Standards are not hard to set; they're challenging to pursue. That is why each colleague you have and each worker you contract needs to purchase toward the objectives you're working and the standards you've set. On the off chance that they don't, you will experience serious difficulties dealing with your group and improving efficiency.

Filing System Organization

Regardless of the amount you endeavor to do on the web and how hard you attempt to work a paperless business, you will need to manage and remain over desk work. Notwithstanding whether you utilize a paper documenting framework or work electronically, it's imperative to build up an efficient framework. How we document and compose our archives enables us to be viable and gainful. Keeping your recording framework written guarantees that everybody in your group can without much of a stretch, sort out, distinguish, and discover data and archives when required. You ought to have two separate envelopes for every property: a month to month receipt organizer and an ace property envelope.

The month to month receipt organizer will have subfolders for solicitations, receipts for gas/oil, electric, water, sewer, first home loan, second home loan, contracts, solicitations, and building grants. The ace property organizer will incorporate both purchasing and selling envelopes and kept in a bolted file organizer. This document contains private data, for example, purchasers' Social Security numbers or the price tag. The entire thought is to rehab properties without doing practically everything yourself. So, when you enlist or expedite your first colleague, this is a simple to follow framework for them to execute and take work off your plate. They need to record and pay the month to month charges in the month to month receipt organizer for your bookkeeping purposes. This framework considers the development and takes you from expert to entrepreneur a great deal sooner and with a versatile framework to execute your bookkeeping and recording.

Post-rehab Accounting

You won't discover numerous real estate investors feeling impatient when doing accounting and bookkeeping. Be that as it may, regardless of whether it isn't some tea, you should know about each watch that comes in, and each look at that goes. I've seen numerous investors get exclusive focus taking a gander at their properties' buy costs, deal costs, and rehab costs. Too many overlook the regular dollar sums and exchanges engaged with utilities, financing charges, shutting expenses, and other holding costs. When you ask them how much benefit they made on a rehab bargain, they can't give you an answer!

There is no reason that you shouldn't realize every dollar spent or made on an arrangement down to the penny. The exact opposite thing you need to happen is to leave the end table, reasoning that you made $30,000 when you just made $10,000. You'll be sure if you're running a professional, successful, productive business. More terrible, you may not know whether you're notwithstanding making a benefit. Your business's prosperity relies upon the benefit of each arrangement, so you must track every exchange down to the penny. Be that as it may, before you begin utilizing bookkeeping programming like QuickBooks, you'll have to comprehend the basics. A bookkeeping framework's total capacity is just sorting out budgetary data and giving precise reports to follow your cash. You don't need to be a specialist, yet you should get comfortable with bookkeeping standards and strategies. Having a piece of working information on bookkeeping before you hand it off to a clerk enables you to finish your own governing rules.

QuickBooks

Generally, you can execute your bookkeeping all around just with QuickBooks.

QuickBooks Pro or QuickBooks Online is anything but complicated to-utilize bookkeeping projects intended to push little to medium-sized organizations know precisely where they stand monetarily and how to be progressively powerful.

The apparatuses monitor client and merchant data utilizing checks, keep a point by point data for every single financial balance in the business, and enable you to run reports. They additionally deal with any stock you have (the properties you purchase and sell).

While there is undoubtedly more than one approach to set up and do, you're representing a rehab and flip business; I will share the framework I've utilized for as long as a decade for following and finishing off a large number of properties.

To keep a precise record of your assets and where your organization stands monetarily, you'll need accounting and bookkeeping frameworks set up for the whole deal, and that can support development. There are various sorts of bookkeeping programming accessible; I like to work with and observe QuickBooks be extremely basic and direct.

Income Statement

The income statement, or benefit and misfortune explanation, abridges your organization's incomes and costs over some undefined time frame. Numerous organizations take a gander at a quarterly or yearly P&L to see their exhibition and perceive whether they are profiting.

Such vast numbers of real estate investors are unfit to address that question on seven days to a week, month to month, or quarterly. A P&L with appropriate detailing will enable you to do that by following your items' benefit by utilizing the income and expenses related to the item (specifically, the house).

As a result of the kind of item you're selling, your P&L will indicate huge spikes each four to a half year when you sell a completed rehab and get a $30,000 to $60,000 rehab benefit.

The expenses regarding the buy of a property will shift and incorporate the sum we buy the property for and the end expenses related to that exchange.

These expenses are altogether promoted and put in our advantage account inside our bookkeeping framework. You would set up a benefit account (we utilized fixed resources for this reason) in your graph of records with the property address.

You'll likewise build up a risk or credit account in the diagram of records with the property address. It would be best to record any obtained assets (regardless of whether new credit or accepted home loan) as an obligation.

Rehab expenses are every one of the costs related to materials and work during the rehab. Rehab costs likewise incorporate all holding expenses. The rehab expenses include anything spent to remodel the property that will remain with the property.

When you spend this cash, you record it in the advantage account you set up when it was obtained. The rehab assets increment the complete estimation of the benefit record and add to the cost premise of your unique buy and securing cost and cost.

Conveying expenses are those expenses acquired to hold the property.

These incorporate any home loan or advance installments for the property, property charges, protection premiums, utility installments (water, power, gas, rubbish, etc.), and garden care (once the rehab is finished, etc.

Selling expenses are the expenses caused to get the property sold commissions, any end costs paid in the purchaser's interest, shutting of sale costs, any home loan or advance adjustments, etc.

This classification additionally incorporates things the purchaser has required as a component of the buy contract.

For instance, if the purchaser needs you to put a fence around the property to close, at that point, you could represent that as a feature of the selling costs.

In any case, if the purchaser requires a particular fix that ought to have been made as a piece of the rehab procedure, I would incorporate it in the rehab costs.

The deal is when we enter a diary sector to discount the all-out equalizations in the advantage and risk records to record the expense of offers, and the returns got as income.

Time To List Your Flip

You've spent a lot of time in the last few months getting yourself to this point. First, you did all the research to find the right area. Then, you spent a considerable amount of time hunting for just the right house. You probably put offers in on some great possibilities and finally purchased one you've renovated to become your flip. Wow, what a journey!

Remember, each home is different, and each area is different. I'm going to show you some ways that I've approached the sales process, and hopefully, you can apply some of them to your flip.

The Importance of Staging

A common question I get is, "Do you stage your homes?" I sometimes do. Many factors come into the scene when deciding to stage or not. The biggest for me is the price point—I still flip many homes priced under $150,000. I've found it difficult to have money in the budget for staging at that price point. I'm not saying it is impossible, but very difficult.

What I typically do for these modest homes is a "light staging." I place towels in the bathroom and kitchen, knick-knacks on the kitchen counters, and maybe a few plants here or there. I might put a small table and chairs in an eat-in kitchen. I love to have a place for prospective buyers to sit and talk about the house during a showing. If they can admire their new kitchen, then all the better!

There is nothing better than a beautifully staged home! So many people have a hard time envisioning what a home will look like when it is vacant. The average person (i.e., husband) sometimes can't see it. Staging is where you can help a prospective buyer if the budget allows. A good stager lays out furniture to make the best use of space and uses the right colors to complement what you've done. When a home is staged correctly, it feels pulled together. It may seem like a lot of money, but staging should be something you fit into your budget when it comes to higher-valued homes.

Listing Your Property

If you have been working with a Realtor, this will most likely be how you list your home. Commissions in our area right now are running 2.5% to 3%. The seller pays real estate commissions at the time of sale. If you agree to a 3% listing agreement, you will pay 6% of your sales price to Realtors, with 3% to the listing agent and 3% to the selling agent. Typically, you will have one agent that lists your property and another agent that brings the buyer. However, it can be the same agent.

I know how hard it can be to build a 3% commission into my business budget. I have some Realtors who offer to do a 2.5% commission, especially when they have multiple listings with me. However, I budget for 3%.

I hear many people gripe about how much Realtors make, but trust me, most I know they don't make a lot of money. People don't think about the number of times Realtors work for free. They can work with a client for weeks or months whose personal circumstances may change while searching for a property, and suddenly they aren't able to buy it.

When there is no sale, there is no commission for the Realtor. That's just part of engaging in the business.

There are some other alternatives to listing with a traditional Realtor, including hybrid models that have popped up over the last few years. One is the "flat fee" model. In it, you will typically work with a licensed Realtor. However, rather than charging a 3% commission, you will pay a flat fee depending on the house's price. Typically, you'll pay one amount for homes selling under $200,000 and another amount for homes selling between $200,000 and $500,000. They all have their specific formula, but this is how they are set up. The flat fee system can be a great alternative to get the services of a full-time Realtor at a discounted rate.

There is another option that may or may not be available where you are. Honestly, most Realtors are opposed to it, so that it may have a limited life in my area also. Realtors can create a

$500 to $1,000 listing for your property in the MLS, but not do much else. This option may be acceptable for a few people out there, but you don't have much access to a Realtor when you have questions that you will look at.

The other possibility is selling without a Realtor at all. It is well known as a "for sale by owner" or FSBO. Unless you are very familiar with real estate and comfortable with all the paperwork, negotiations, etc., I would not recommend going this route; granted, you could save some money, but it may not be worth it—you'll be all on your own.

If you go the FSBO route, numerous websites specialize in this and help guide you through the process. Most also can supply you with any signage and paperwork that you may need. There are many these sites out there; see what each has to offer, what others have to say about them, and then make your decision.

Another topic that many people feel strongly about is hosting open houses. I know Realtors who are adamant that it is a waste of their time. They believe that four hours could be spent doing so many more things that could sell your home quicker. I understand this argument, and it may be so for some; however, I've had good luck with open houses. I feel like any exposure to potential buyers is a plus. Yes, maybe most don't turn into that buyer for the house being held open, but they may—you never know.

There's the thought process that the only people who show up to open houses are the neighbors. What's wrong with that? As I said earlier, I've sold more than one house due to interest from my neighbors—you don't know who they tell about it. All of a sudden, you may be getting a call from one of their cousins who wanted to see your property!

One last thing that I have found with open houses I've got more interested in my other flip projects from people attending an open house. I can't say for sure that I have ever sold another home to them, but I know of a few people who follow us on Facebook after attending to see if we'll do things in areas they are interested in. Can I prove I've sold homes this way? No, but I know it sure can't hurt! Whether or not to host open houses is up to you—you know how I feel, but that's a discussion to have with your Realtor.

An important topic is what you list your home for now that you are ready to sell. I have that number in my head before I even make an offer on the house, and you too. However, things can change through the time you purchase, renovate, and sell again. It's hope for the better, but if it isn't, you'll need to know that too.

Get with your Realtor and pull new comparables, as there could easily be recent sales in the last two or three months, and you need to know about them. If you've done your renovations as I suggested, you should be thinking about pushing the market. See what the high end for your type of home is and shoot for that. I'll make my numbers work (hopefully) with a lower ARV, so if it sells for the higher number, then that's the gravy!

Remember that there is a fine line here and let your Realtor help guide you. If you labeled the price of your home too high, you may not get any traffic, and it could sit. You don't want that! Also, ask yourself if it will appraise. It doesn't matter what you get it under contract for—if they are obtaining financing, then it needs to appraise. It is where it helps to have a relationship with an appraiser. I always make sure that I have the comparables to show an appraiser that the sales price is justifiable.

Once, I bought a small, two-bedroom townhouse. When I was researching it, I saw that the highest two-bedroom sale in the last twelve months was $112,900. I knew that mine would be nicer than that one, so I felt like I could push it a little higher, but any more than that would be hard for an appraiser. Most lenders want comparables to be what they call "bracketed," meaning they want to see a sale lower than your sales price and one higher than your sales price. I didn't have that, but there were homes with another half bath that had sold higher. My thoughts were that an appraiser could use one of those to have a higher sale and then make a positive adjustment for mine, which had more updates.

What ended up happening was a little unusual. I listed the property at $116,900, knowing that I was pushing it and that there was a possibility that it wouldn't appraise. We had multiple offers in the first forty-eight hours, all of which were good. However, one was great—$118,900 and a quick cash close. With a cash offer, appraisals are not typically requested, as lenders aren't worried about the loan value since it is cash. I jumped on this one, and we ended up closing in less than two weeks!

I told the Realtor that the residents of this complex needed to thank me. Many times, the values in condos and townhome complexes take a little while to appreciate. Many units are of similar square footage and design, making it difficult for appraisers to meet sales prices higher than the most recent highest. You can circumvent that when you have a cash sale! I told her that I just raised the value of two-bedroom units by a little over 5%. You're welcome!

Do I Lower My Price If My Home Not Getting The Interest?

Many people ask this question, and every house is different, but my general tendency is not to wait a long time. In this business, time is money, and I'd prefer to lower something, get it sold, and move on to the subsequent project.

Now don't get me wrong, I'm not talking about giving it away, but about dropping the price sooner.

A lot of variables can affect that decision. Are you getting a lot of traffic? Make sure it's the price and not something else that you can correct.

You will love to get feedback from as many showings as possible.

You can receive a wealth of information! Not everyone will be honest, but with enough feedback, you can see common issues that you may be able to address sooner. It is easier than ever for agents to get feedback once they have shown the property with so much automated now.

Neal Hooper

Managing Multiple Flips

You can have a small amount of overlap between two rounds or perform five games simultaneously. Either way, you need to develop effective strategies to keep

everything in order and keep pace with each project. Even if there are five projects in progress, you can only make money after selling the house. Therefore, please concentrate on completing and selling the house as soon as possible.

Consider Location

If you want to manage multiple changes, you need to travel frequently between properties, houses, and inventory stores. You can choose between two primary strategies. You can intentionally search for homes close to each other or search for houses that meet your criteria, regardless of location. Although none of these strategies are incredibly wrong, it is essential always to maintain a particular state. Therefore, even if you want to find a house nearby, don't deviate from the upcoming city's ideal property.

Benefits of Group Activities

The most significant advantage of group features is that they are close to each other. You can quickly move between houses to monitor progress. If there is a problem with one house, you can get there quickly from another house. You can also save time and even delivery costs. Notifying the delivery company that the residences are indeed close to each other can be used as a basis for negotiating delivery charges or delivery time. Using the same contractor on multiple properties will make it easier for the contractor to stay in touch with the two projects and transfer workers between projects if necessary. It is good to keep attributes close to each other.

Disadvantages of Grouping Properties

There are two main disadvantages to following this strategy. The first disadvantage is that it will remove many potentially great features. As mentioned earlier, you want to try to keep your choices open when looking for a house. Its fundamental goal is to maximize and protect your profits. It partly means that you will find large businesses and houses that require minimal renovation. You may not find different attributes that are close to each other.

Second, if the renovation is completed in a short time, you will have several properties on the market simultaneously. It may create unnecessary competition among potential buyers between houses. One way to reduce this shortcoming is to arrange the purchase time so that the renovation can be completed at a different time. You can also use it to your advantage so that potential buyers can see the other houses you are selling. You might sell one of them.

Negotiate Different Contracts

For each house you invest in, you have to negotiate a purchase and sale contract. Moving multiple houses generates a lot of paperwork and a lot of mental work. The project must be organized. Mixing in different houses can cause severe errors in the negotiation process. In addition to staying organized and keeping documents organized, having a broker will help you immensely. Hiring a manager or office assistant can also help. Although you can start on your own, multiple managing circles are intricate, and you are unlikely to handle it yourself. Before jumping to the different attributes, you can consider your options. Even if you don't have an office, you can still hire a virtual assistant to keep your documents and documents up to date.

Bulk Quotation

If you want to buy multiple properties at once, consider buying multiple properties from the same bank or seller. It provides you with a trading point. You can share various attributes as part of the offer. The quotation you prepare can include a "bulk-free" discount to purchase all items at once. Although this may seem unconventional, it is not uncommon.

Organize Paperwork

Even if you reach a volume contract for multiple properties, each property will have its agreement and sales documents. It is essential to organize it separately to allocate all income and expenses to the correct property. It is necessary to determine the profit of each property as well as the time for taxation.

Organize Multiple Timetables

For each property you change, you must follow the renovation schedule. According to each house's starting distance and the renovation required, he will simultaneously supervise multiple teams and projects. The important thing is to write out each timeline in detail. Once the supplier, repair, or delivery is planned, it needs to be written down.

How To Maintain And Locate Multiple Packages

You can do something to maintain and track multiple timelines. The first thing you can do is keep everything on the calendar. Although you might want to keep a calendar for each attribute, it can be even more confusing. Use a planner that allows you to view monthly and weekly views. Then, you can choose the highlight color to coordinate each attribute. Write everything down on the calendar and highlight it in a color that matches each appointment's theme.

To keep multiple due dates, another thing you can do is to set reminders daily using the online calendar app. If you need to have a meeting at home, it will remind you of the day's meeting or appointment.

Finally, one thing you want to do is join the hotel every day.

Contact the contractor to understand the development of the day and achievements. If you have multiple houses working simultaneously, it is best to work directly for you on each property. Not only can they stay in touch 24 hours a day, but they can also provide daily progress reports and the latest information on renewal, delivery, etc.

Coordinate Contractors to Work In Multiple Homes.

Discuss with your contractor what needs to be done for each property. If you plan to have the same contractor work on multiple properties, please schedule with him immediately after you have the keys to each property. If your contractor sends out as many notices as possible, they will likely work with you.

Keep Up to Date with Different Pojects.

The easiest way to track multiple items is to not aggregate content. If you must perform a function, do so. If you want to buy materials, please go and buy it. Submit your paperwork every night. Go to all the property every day. Call back as soon as possible and register with the contractor every day. You cannot stop procrastinating.

In addition to coordinating and tracking multiple timelines, you also need to coordinate and track multiple budgets. Each family has its budget, and expenditure must be monitored separately to determine profit and expenditure correctly. When to submit taxes, your accountant wants to know which house each type of expense can be allocated to. When registering for tax, keeping an eye on costs can save a lot of time and money. You can save money by reducing the time that must be paid to the accountant. The longer the accountant spends, the more it consumes.

Maintain and Track Multiple Budgets

It is essential to keep a project folder for each household you are dealing with to keep everything organized. As part of this folder, you can put a large envelope in the front pocket to collect receipts during the day. It will prevent the receipt from being lost. The disadvantage of this method is that you can purchase items for several houses on one receipt. At the end of each day, check the envelope and letter costs in the corresponding budget. Check the receipt and highlight the items to be sent to different homes.

How To Save Money On Multiple Projects

Saving a lot of money is a relatively simple way to save money. You can order directly from the supplier and order many items that can be used in each household. For example, light switch covers, new switches, lights, lights, and screws are examples of household items and purchased bulk.

Tax Registration and Payment

Fortunately, relocation will increase your annual income, but you still need to register for a house purchase even if necessary. Even if you do not make any profit, all factors must be considered. In addition to recording everything, you also need to group everything. For example, you can't just ask for a fee and add a number. You must be able to divide the total based on the actual expenditures incurred.

Document Interview

All expenses on all receipts must be kept. Unless you can prove where and when you spent the money, you cannot claim deductions. If you lose income, you will lose deductions, which will cost you money. The deduction will be deducted from the total amount applied to you.

If there is no deduction, you will pay more taxes. It is essential to record all receipts and expenses.

Hire an Accountant

As you start to act, your tax filing obligations will increase dramatically. You need to have a thorough understanding of tax laws and expectations; otherwise, you may end up spending a lot of money. You may have paid too much tax, but you may also pay a fine for late order, wrong paperwork, or any other mistake. The best way is to hire an accountant. Look for an accountant who works with regular investors and understands the business. If you can find an accountant with real estate investment experience, so much the better.

Know When You Need Extra Help

When you reach the point where you can simultaneously have multiple transmissions, you will be attracted to different directions.

It will soon be difficult for you to handle everything yourself. Although you have increased your expenses, you can help you increase efficiency and productivity by hiring people.

The first thing you need to know is what kind of people you need to hire. A good starting point is to find out exactly where you want to spend time on exercise.

Ask yourself the following questions:

1.   What are your business advantages?

2.   Which tasks do you like best?

3.   What task will make you feel best?

4.   Even if it takes a long time, what tasks do you want to perform?

If you answer these questions honestly, you will determine your real strengths.

Although most people think that your strengths are just what you are good at, it is a combination of what you are good at and what you like best. If you don't like a task, you will often delay time and work inefficiently.

After listing the tasks to be responsible, list all the tasks that must be performed. Divide these tasks into categories that can be achieved by one person. For example, if you have a long list of tasks, they belong to the clergy, accounting, messaging, etc. In the fall, you can hire an assistant to handle all these tasks. If you don't want to monitor the team, you can hire a team leader to supervise the daily overhaul and make sure everything goes according to plan. If you only carry out small house repairs but want to free up time to focus on the business, you can hire a house-to-house maintenance team to complete smaller renovation tasks.

How to Price and Prepare Rentals

Determining Rental Rates and Security Deposit Amounts

One of the most important skills you must have in successfully managing your rental property is collecting rent. You will need to determine how much

rent should be charged, ensure your tenants pay rent on time, and establish how much will be charged for security deposits. You must also be aware of when and if you can raise rental rates to cover cost increases.

Landlords and property managers may collect funds other than rent for various reasons, based on local law. It typically takes the form of advance rent to protect landlords if the tenant vacates the property without providing notice. A security deposit may also be charged to cover any damage that may be incurred by a tenant. While local law may allow a landlord or property manager to charge these fees, there are usually strict procedures. In some areas, the local laws require that the tenant be provided with dated receipts for every payment.

Your goal is to set the rent at the highest rate possible to help cover all of your costs, and ultimately, leave you with some money in your pocket. However, you don't want to set the rent so high that it becomes hard to find an interested tenant. Doing this could cause you to leave the property vacant, which could cost you thousands of dollars in the long run. Below are the steps you can take to do your market research to determine how high you will set the rent.

You will also want to find out which rental properties ended up lowering or raising their rates. You can do this by contacting the landlords of the properties you formerly visited and tell them that you are still interested in the property. Inform them that you are still looking at other properties but want to see if they are still available and whether they are offering the same rate.

You will also want to consider the trends in how much rent has gone up/down in the area. You hope to find a location where rental rates are going up due to high demand in the area. It will give you an idea of what rental income you can receive in the future.

At this point, you should have a fairly good idea of the amount of rent you will be able to charge. However, if you are new at renting properties, you may want to get other professionals' opinions to see what rate they believe you can get for rent at the property.

Throw out any prices that seem either much higher or much lower than the median for similar properties. You are not looking to be the cheapest property on the market; you are just looking to be slightly below most properties that are the closest match to yours.

The right rent amount will help you make a profit off your income investment and allow you to pay bills and lead a better life, as you intended to. The right rent amount will also make sense to the tenant and reasonable enough to be content paying over a long time.

Setting a standard price for all one-bedroom apartments will make little sense, especially if they are not the same.

Unless the units are all similar, this strategy will only hurt you. Charge different rates based on the unit's desirability.

When the economy is bad, rental rates often go up because people can no longer afford the mortgages that come with owning a home. It usually forces them to rent. A suffering economy may also lead to smaller, cheaper apartments in more demand because people have to downsize to cut costs. Think about the summer as well. The demand for larger apartments will usually be higher since many families are looking to move in time for the school year.

Have your eye on the market at all times. Understand the trends and adapt to them accordingly. In addition to drawing tenants to you, this will make it possible to succeed in a financial sense.

The rule of thumb here is that you are free to charge higher rent when your unit's demand is high. However, when the demand is low, lower rental rates may be necessary to attract tenants.

Setting Competitive Rates

When determining the amount of money that should be charged for rental rates, it is important to make sure you have covered all operating expenses, while also allowing enough left over for a reasonable return on your investment. At the same time, you must make sure the rates you set are competitive. Of course, the ideal situation would be for a landlord to set the rental amount at whatever amount is necessary for them to cover major expenses and earn a profit at the same time.

However, it must be understood that local laws in some areas can regulate rental rates. You must also consider local competition as well.

The simple fact is that if the amount that you charge is higher than what other landlords and property managers in the local area are charging, you will likely find it difficult to locate desirable tenants. You may still be able to rent out the property, but the tenants that are attracted to the property may be the types that are frequently late with the rent. You must make certain that the rental rates you charge are competitive enough so that you can attract desirable tenants and ensure your property remains occupied.

The amount you charge for rent should never be based on simply what you have heard or assumptions. You must research and find out how many tenants in the area are paying in rent. There are many ways you can do this, including by perusing the rental ads online and in the local newspapers. You can also speak with neighbors in the area to find out what the going rental rates are. Based on what you find out, you can then begin to set a competitive rental rate. Keep in mind that you must also make sure you know any local rental control laws that may dictate your charge.

Increasing Rents

Generally speaking, you will not be able to raise rents if you have a signed lease with your tenant. When the lease expires, you may then increase the rent. Usually, the only exception to this is if you have a clause in the lease that allows you to raise the rent sooner. The lease will typically specify the amount of time you must give in the prior notice before you can raise the rent. Local, state, or provincial law may also require you to give a certain amount of notice before you are allowed to increase the rent.

Remember that even if local laws and the lease do not require you to give a certain amount of notice, it can still be a good idea to provide tenants with a month or two of advance written notice before issuing any rent increases. If your tenant rents on a month-to-month basis, you will typically be able to increase the rent as often as you like, provided that you issue the amount of notice that is required by law. If there are rent control laws in your area, there may also be limits regarding how frequently you can increase the rent.

Deciding on Your Rental Policies

Before deciding on your policies, however, you must first get familiar with your local landlord laws. Different states, counties, and cities will have their regulations. Do your homework. The fastest way to get in trouble in court is to have a clause ruled illegal because it contradicts local laws.

Collecting Security Deposits

States, provinces, and even some local ordinances may regulate security deposits. Landlords and property managers may wish to collect a security deposit, if permissible by local law. The security deposit can be used for covering damage that may occur in a rental property beyond normal wear and tear. State, provincial or local law may limit the amount charged for a security deposit in some areas.

The term 'damage' often refers to tears or rips in the flooring, holes in the walls or ceilings, major stains, burns in the countertops, missing items, damaged screens or blinds, etc.

Damage usually does not cover or include normal discoloration, rust, worn carpeting, loose grouting, hard water stains in the bathroom, cracked or chipped paint, etc.

For the most part, local laws will allow landlords and property owners to collect security deposits based specifically on the damage covered by the deposit. Local laws may also state how and when portions of the deposits not used must be returned.

The conditions and terms must be clearly stated in the rental or lease agreement.

Landlords and property owners are usually required in most areas to place security deposits they collect in an escrow account and provide the tenant with any interest accrued by the deposit. In some areas, the amount of interest that must be paid on the security deposit is specified.

When collecting a security deposit, it can be a good idea to have all new tenants complete a checklist, such as the one below, when they move in that describes the property's condition.

When the tenant moves out, you can use this checklist for determining any damage that may have been done to the property.

Collecting Advance Rent

Some landlords and property owners may choose to collect advance rent to cover the lease's last month.

Advance rent can help offset rental income that might be lost if a tenant moves out without notice.

In some areas, you may be allowed to count the last month's rent as a portion of the security deposit. It means that you can use part of it for repairs or cleaning. In a few areas, the use of the last month's rent is restricted to its stated purpose and cannot be used for anything else. If you use those funds for cleaning or repairs, you could violate local law.

Collecting Monthly Rental Payments

Most rental agreements and leases clearly state the due date each month for the rent and where payments must be made.

Before renting out a property, you will need to determine which type of payment will be acceptable for you, such as cash, money order, or check. If you decide you will require a certain type of payment, you may state this in the lease. Most landlords and property managers issue a written and dated receipt when they collect cash payments. The receipt should state the name of the tenant as well as the amount paid. In some areas, local law may require that you issue a written receipt even when payments are made by personal check or money order.

Exit & Contingency Planning

The rental business is fun, fast, and potentially quite profitable. But it's a business, and like all businesses, your experience will include some wonderful moments of guest interaction, financial growth and prosperity, capital appreciation, and learning opportunities.

Similarly, you'll also experience some not-so-wonderful moments of long work hours, a part-time job you can't easily quit, guests that don't check out on time, cleaners that didn't show up, angry and difficult guests, leaky water heaters, broken furnishings, negative analyses, declining property values and rising HOA expenses. If you haphazardly enter the market without a plan, you may also face evictions, loan defaults, foreclosure, and ultimately bankruptcy.

Fortunately, if you have a solid plan, then these last few items are quite rare, even if your plan doesn't turn out to be fully accurate. Given the possibilities, the decision to enter the vacation rental market shouldn't be taken lightly.

Most of us have day jobs working at a company we don't own. If the business crumbles, you're out a job, but you can find another similar one at the succeeding company without much loss.

Similarly, if you just get sick of the work, you can walk away with two weeks' notice and never come back. When you manage your vacation rental, you don't have these luxuries.

You are the business, and if the business crumbles (bankruptcy), your financial life may crumble with it. You can't just walk away, at least not easily or immediately. You can sell the property, hire a professional manager, or just stop offering rentals and turn it into a vacation home, but these take time and cost money. You should always understand the risks and the implications of entering this market before you do so.

While it's important to discuss the negatives, it's not our intent to paint a picture of doom and gloom. While it's relatively uncommon to see someone enter the market, which shouldn't, it's far more common to see someone not entering the market, which should.

We talk to many people, "I wish I could do that," but then never do.

Some go so far as to find a property, run the numbers and then get cold feet at the last minute. Some simply assume they don't make enough money to finance a second home purchase but never walk into a bank and try. Others worry about the time commitment in self-managing, while some worry they may not find renters.

These are all valid concerns, and only you can make the final decision to pull the trigger. But in our experience, we haven't met many people that took the plunge and regretted it.

To be sure, there have been a few of these people – generally bad investments, properties that didn't cash flow as predicted, properties with hidden damage, or even couples suddenly surprised with a child and who no longer have the time for active property management. In short, life happens.

Rather than focusing on the negatives and letting those negatives talk you out of your decision, focus on the positives that can happen while planning for how to deal with the negatives should they occur.

It can be a simple budgetary countermeasure to combat a specific one-off issue, such as an unforeseen major repair. Or it can be a phased or complete exit plan to remove yourself from the business if need be.

We encourage everyone who enters this business to have an exit plan, even if you don't expect to execute it, because you likely won't want to manage your vacation rental until the day you die. At some point, you'll want to transition out of your business, and the sooner you think about it, the easier it'll be to execute on your exit strategy when you're ready.

Your exit strategy can be staged as a progressive withdrawal from the business, or it can be a comprehensive exit strategy where you sell off the property and walk away. You can also have plans for both.

A real exit plan is conceptually rather simple: list the house for sale, and when it sells, you're out of the business. In practice, it's not usually that easy.

For example, it may not be a quick sale depending on the market conditions, or you may walk away with a loss even if your property has appreciated (due to agent's commissions and your initial investment in furnishings, repairs, and renovations that may dwarf any profit you've made). But you're likely to walk away with a profit if your property has appreciated, or if you've owned it long enough for most of the initial furnishings to be depreciated off your records already and have a history of good cashflow.

Many people experiencing significant capital appreciation make the unexpected decision to walk away just because it's a good opportunity to realize a capital profit – either upgrading to a larger rental home, cashing out and enjoying the money, or investing in something else (like a different business).

We usually don't coach people to purchase vacation rentals just for appreciation but rather to invest for cash flow. When significant appreciation happens, however, certainly don't look that gift horse in the mouth!

The thing to remember with a total exit is that you should always continue to take care of all guests you have recorded until someone else has been appointed to take care of them for you (mainly, the new owner).

Don't leave your guests hanging just because you're exiting the business. It's good karma and good human behavior to see through what you've started, since someone else's vacation is riding on your actions. Make the transition smooth and painless.

A staged or phased exit is slightly different from a total exit, and it can take on several different forms. It is synonymous with contingency planning in its earliest stages, and in its final stage, it may be a total exit.

A staged exit can either be a response to a situation due to factors beyond your control (such as regulatory compliance), or it can be an intentional move to reduce the time you invest in your rental business.

Consider an intentional phased exit. When you first purchase the property, you may be self-managing because you're high on time and low on cash, trying to build a strong reserve fund, and wanting to learn the business by doing all of the work. As your cash position changes (you build your reserve, refinance to lower payments, or pay off the mortgage completely), you may find that your profit is growing higher and higher, and your free time smaller and smaller.

At some point, your time is becoming more valuable than your profit, but you're not ready to sell your properties and call it quits.

You may hire a professional property manager. It can be the first stage to exit, whereby you're no longer dealing with reservations, guests, and maintenance. Your profitability will decrease because you're paying someone to do work you were doing yourself already. You need to decide what's worth more: your time or your money. With your new-found free time, you can pursue other ventures – acquiring new properties, spending time with your family, working more at your day job, or perhaps even writing a record on your own Airbnb successes!

Another phased exit plan could be growing your rental portfolio to include fewer but larger houses. By starting with more small, lower-cost properties, you can eventually trade- up to fewer larger properties. It means fewer places to manage (although each may be more complex than a small property, generally, the workload is smaller with fewer places).

Perhaps you've bought two homes at $125,000 each and paid them off over time. You then have the option to trade them for a single

$250,000 home with no mortgage. Phase-out by trading up; you'll reduce your workload and get good tax benefits along the way.

Finally, regulatory concerns may drive you to execute a phased exit plan. If you're managing vacation rentals and your HOA passes a new rule banning transient rentals, you may be forced to step back to monthly rentals. For every property we buy, we ask about 100 questions that start with "What happens if..." We then look at what's going on in the local, state, and national economy and we plan accordingly.

In some states, short-term rentals are still quite new, and investors are still learning how to co-exist with residents.

It creates additional risks for the investor. Suppose the investor's business model relies on short-term rentals to cash flow (a situation everyone reading this volume is likely in), and legislation eliminates the short-term rental market. In that case, your business plan can flop very quickly without a backup plan. A well-prepared investor will know their financial situation for their second (and maybe third and fourth) the best course of action. Its contingency plan can then be executed readily should such a situation arise. Such a plan might include conversion from short-term to a monthly vacation rental or a long-term rental, or even selling the property. If you know what your options are upfront and have the budgets done already, you'll be much more prepared for a quick reaction than anyone else in your area, and you'll get the first-to-market advantage when you have to execute on your backup plan.

Handling Crises

Natural disasters, illness, housing bubble bursts, and unforeseen property repairs are things you need to plan for and be prepared to handle. The 2020 Coronavirus (COVID-19) brings home how illness can affect the world, negatively. But the examples can go farther back.

In 1918, the flu infected 500 million people. Worldwide 50 million deaths occurred, with 675,000 cases in the United States, according to the CDC. During this time, people were also dying because of World War I (1914-1918). After the war and flu, the Great Depression affected the US and globally wrecked the foreign exchange system. World War II continued to wreak havoc on the economy. Then the

Korean War happened, followed by the Vietnam War, and a recession in the '80s. Nearly every decade has a crisis, whether it is natural or not. The 2000s started with 9-11 and over-inflated home prices.

The housing boom that burst in 2007 took the world more than four years to recover, and even then, issues remained until more recently, the housing market turned around. According to the Guardian, a UK newspaper, flooding and heavy rains increased in the last decade to more than 50% what it used to be, which means natural disasters have affected the economy. Asia, Africa, and the Midwest United States have all suffered economically from floods. If hurricanes and typhoons are added, Japan, Florida, and the Gulf Coast felt the impact in these first 20 years of the new millennium. Even New England had to deal with a deadly winter storm requiring disaster relief.

The point of listing this history from the world wars up to now is to show you that nearly every decade, something has impacted the United States or the World, negatively, and thus changed the economic standing of the areas most affected.

The United States Dollar was finally strengthening world currencies like the Canadian Dollar, Great British Pound, and the Euro, but it has weakened again. The stock market has seen huge drops, and people with investments have lost thousands, if not their entire retirement fund. All property investments are affected by the 2020 Pandemic, and lessons can be learned from the choices being made by the President, his staff, and individual state Governors to help you plan for future issues that may arise.

Deficits Grow

Every country in the world will see economic changes. Countries currently showing deficits will see these increase, while those in positive situations may decrease to the point of having a deficit. Disaster relief must come from somewhere, and one solution posed by the US is to have the Federal Reserve print money. When this occurs, the dollar weakens because the money appeared from thin air. The Federal Reserve already decreased interest rates to help banks ride the tide, impacting the deficit due to asset-backed securities being depleted to cover the banks.

Businesses Closed, States Closed

The pandemic led to stores closing, many probably permanently. States have closed, and the National Guard, FEMA, and CDC have all deployed to maintain order and reduce the number of people affected.

People are either out of occupations or working from home due to business closures. Many small businesses never offered sick pay, health insurance, or vacation pay. Service industries also lack these attributes; only a small amount of the world population is making income.

With talks of printing money for each US legal resident and creating bills to help all businesses, the economy may need a decade to recover.

Governor Movements

The Federal Government can only do so much with its power. Much of the authority regarding business and State border closures are held with the Governors of those locations. Colorado is one state that has closed the National Park, requested that all non-essential businesses reduce staff by 50%, and closed restaurants except for takeout, delivery, and drive-thru operations. All at-risk facilities, such as nursing homes, assisted living, and hospitals, require their staff to call, answer a questionnaire, and have their temperature taken before going inside.

Governors are also setting up procedures for real estate, including requests made to rental property investors.

Please note, while it may not apply to all disasters, the information is designed to help you see what can occur and going forward how you might address any situation that arises. For example, in Colorado, the Governor requested landlords to stop eviction procedures and stated that law enforcement would not enforce evictions. The request included allowing for renters to pay late without paying late fees. In the time of need, the Governor wanted landlords to forgive potential late or missed payments and worked to pass legislation that would help the owners to weather the storm regarding missed income. While loans need to be paid, all loan companies, including mortgage places, are asked to stop foreclosure proceedings and defer payments.

Yes, things will be paid back, interest will accrue, but when income is not coming in, the Governor asked for leniency. From these requests, rental property investors can determine a course of action and further use this pandemic to devise a plan for any new potential situation.

Disaster Planning 101

Historical events and how we've dealt with them help you create contingency plans. What would you do if you could not evict people who have not paid you for two months before an issue like the COVID-19 virus?

What if you recently bought a property, using most of your cash flow, and your income slows down? It does not matter whether you are in a flood, tornado, hurricane, earthquake, or ice storm area; you want to have a plan to deal with something if it happens.

The government systems do send aid; however, it is usually a short accounting of what you truly need. Second, insurance companies can take more than a month to process a claim when affected by a natural disaster, fire, or other problem, like a burst pipe.

There is no hard and fast rule for how to manage your property investment business, except to ensure you have a reliable cash flow. But here are some things you might consider when planning.

Analyze government help based on the types of disasters that may occur. For example, floods are covered under insurance policies, and other than clean up funds, the government may not offer small business assistance. The newest virus required a more significant response. However, it takes time for the administration to decide on relief policies.

Analyze your insurance policy. Does it cover you for natural disasters, fires, and other issues? Where does the company draw the line? Some things considered an "act of God" are not always protected.

For example, if you live in a flood plain in Colorado, you may find only one or two companies cover your home.

What are projections is you have a quarter, half, or three-quarters of your tenants paying versus full tenancy? How much do you need to make from rental income to break even?

This last point is imperative to your disaster planning lesson because it determines how long you can exist if you lack rent payments. If you planned appropriately during the purchase phase of your property, you should have this information readily available.

For example, if you have a loan for $350,000 with a payment of $2,500, and you only own one property, you need a hundred percent of the rental income to cover your business.

If you have an apartment complex, with a half-million-dollar loan, a current salary of $400,000, and a loan payment of $100,000, then you can afford to have a lower vacancy or payment rate until the crisis is over.

You will want to speak with each tenant. Send out an email or other written communication. It should read similar to this:

We (the company name) understand tough times are being faced.

We would like to do everything we can to help. If you are currently struggling or may face problems soon, please contact our office, and we will work to find a solution that best fits the situation.

Making a statement that you understand and want to hear from tenants helps them contact you to see what you are willing to do. You also invite the tenants to come to you on a case-by-case basis rather than making a blanket statement about the help you are ready to provide.

If one person has six months of rental income, plus monthly expenses saved, then they should be able to ride the tide. A person living paycheck- to-paycheck may not have anything in reserve and will see their income dry up the longer it takes to get back to work or unemployment.

Arrangements such as cutting the rent in half, so you still see something is an option to suggest to tenants.

On the other hand, if you already have a few tenants who are not consistent in their payments, you were considering eviction and want them out, you may not offer a deal.

You might tell this type of tenant, you understand, the government is asking for leeway, but suggest "you" start looking for a new place that you can afford; meanwhile, you are keeping an accurate accounting of what they owe. You have to make it clear that you are only doing what you must under law.

Not only that but from your end, if the government is willing to cover your lost income because you are not able to evict someone, you need to know what you are owed.

There are certain times when you may not be able to make income at all from the property. When a home or apartment complex is affected by a flood or fire, everyone may need to move-out and find a new place while repairing everything.

Yet, you are still liable for any loan you have. Legally, you want to check with each state to determine what you might need to do to help your tenants.

Natural disasters may not require you to help tenants find new living arrangements; however, a fire started by a tenant might require you to help by returning security deposits. Make sure you conduct due diligence to know what your obligations are before you offer anything.

Hopefully, you have learned a little about planning for an event beyond your control from the above. There will always be variables, and the takeaway is to make sure you keep enough cash flow to get you through at least a year of tough times. As you scale your company, step back from the day-to- day, and add new properties, keep in mind what could happen.

Your management staff should also be in on the discussions, if you have one, to help you determine the best policies.

Use Time Management for Your Benefit

When you are doing any type of project, it is always a good idea to do your best to manage your time so that you will be able to get the most out of the time

that you spend on a project. You should make sure that you manage your time as wisely as possible when flipping houses or working on investment properties. It will help you be more successful with your time and increase your flipping homes' profit margin.

Work on Big Projects First

One of the first rules of time management is to tackle the daunting tasks first so that the smaller tasks will feel minor in comparison. If you make sure that you work on the big house projects first, you will be more prepared for the smaller things. Bonus: some of the smaller things may get done while working on bigger projects out of necessity.

If you have something like plumbing or electrical that needs to be replaced, your contractors do that first. It will be one of the biggest parts of the project and will likely require you to tear down portions of the inside of the house. If you start with these, you can avoid having to tear down walls that you just pained or installed new cabinetry in. By doing these big things first, you will make sure that you don't have to backtrack on the work you did or have to redo it since you had to tear walls down completely.

While it may be tempting because it can make a huge difference in a home, don't ever start with the painting. The paint on your home should be the last thing done and should be done by contracted painters. Even when you are at the very end of your project, you do not know if you will have to pull an outlet out of a wall or make adjustments on a wall that was just painted. By making paint the last thing you do, you will save yourself some grief at the project's end.

Set a Time Limit

Each part of the home should have a time limit on it. Your contractor will probably set a time limit for his people to be done in each area of the home but keep in mind that they will probably go over that time limit.

By setting your time limit, you will be prepared when they go on their own. Consider adding around 10% of the time that it aids that it would be done with a project. For example, if your contractor says that a project will be done in 10 days, add an extra day on so that you won't be sorely disappointed when they go over.

The more homes you invest in, the more likely you will know whether a time limit will be realistic. Talk with your contractor before they start on the home and get their idea of the length of time the work will take. They will have the best idea because they are accustomed to doing work like that, and they know how long it takes each of their subcontractors to do the work for them.

If things do not get done in a certain amount of time, push your contractor to get his crews to work more efficiently. There is always work that can be done. Your general contractor should be working as hard as possible to get this done as quickly as possible. As long as you have let him or her know that you are trying to flip the property, they should know that your profit (and their payment) depends on how quickly they can get things done. A time limit will help them know that they are under pressure to get things done as quickly as possible.

Create a Contingency Time Budget

You have a contingency budget for your finances, so why not have one for the time that is going to be spent on the project? Adding expected time to the project will make an overdue project less of a blow on the stress you will already have surrounding the home and the flipping process. If you have a contingency in place for a time, you will use that when your contractors let you know that they will not get things done as quickly as what you thought they were originally going to get it done.

The contingency time budget will work wonders for the stress you feel when you are flipping homes. Your contractors may not know that you have built a few extra days in, but you will know that. They will continue to work hard, but you will have the satisfaction of knowing that you will have extra time if something goes wrong.

One of the easiest ways to do this is to schedule your open house around two weeks after your contractor's expected end date. If the project is done before, simply move your open house up, which is much easier than pushing it back.

Work with Contractors

You don't necessarily need to get down and dirty with the contractors working on your home but do everything you can to help them out with the project. If they need permits, give them the information they need to take to the city. If they need paperwork from you, make it a priority. Your contractor is trying to work as quickly as possible so that your project will get done as quickly as possible. Don't make their job harder.

If there are small things that you can do to help the contractor, like carrying in supplies for painters or helping to screw on electrical outlet plates, do it. You may be paying for them to do everything regarding the renovation, but nothing says you can't help. Remember, the more bodies the contractors have done work, the faster the project will get done. If your project gets done before you were planning, you will make more profits on it and much more quickly than what you have set out to do.

Even though your contractor is technically hired help, you should not treat them as such. You should be a team player and work with them to ensure that things are getting done the right way. There are many things that you will be able to do to help out your contractor. Simply ask them if there is anything that you can do to help get the project done quickly.

Consider a Project Manager

One of the easiest things you can do to manage your time is to get someone else to do it for you. A project manager is that person, and they will be able to provide you with the help you need when it comes to handling your contractor and everything else throughout the renovation.

A professional project manager will assess your renovation situation and take things over for you. The only thing you will need to do is sign off on major changes and, initially, let the project manager know what you want to do to the house while working on it.

Make sure that you only hire a project manager when you are ready. A manager can be expensive and can eat into the budget that you have set for your flip. If you are just getting started with flipping houses and investment properties, you probably don't need a project manager. Try your hardest to manage your time on your own and make sure that you are doing things the right way. Once you have flipped many houses, have made a lot of money, and have more than one property you are working on at a time, you may want to consider hiring a project manager for each of your investment properties.

How Today's Technology Can Keep You Informed

Technology Can Change Your Real Estate Business

Technology has infiltrated many industries, and real estate is one of them. All participants –agents, home buyers, and home sellers – and it has been for the better.

As a real estate investor, the most challenging part of the business is how competitive the market is and how you need to employ every available weapon to build your business. Using available new technology is one of the best ways to do this.

The following are some of the ways real estate investors can boost their business by leveraging technology.

Property Search

When it comes to searching for properties, the Internet comes into play leveled the playing field. In the past, it took an expert to determine when and where new properties became available and figure out homes sales that were comparable for that specific area.

However, today, this information is instantaneous with a couple of clicks. Finding For Sale properties is incredibly simple by using any credible real estate website. If you're looking for FSBO (for sale by owner) properties, Craigslist is a good website that can be fruitful, and Auction.com is a good site for deals if you lean towards foreclosures.

As an investor, you can scale your portfolio using technology with free online education, the availability of sales comps, rental estimates, and access to online deals, and simple ways to evaluate the deal.

Sales Comps Availability

Zillow is a great website for investors who are savvy and looking to work up CMAs in minutes.

Rental Estimates

Zillow has a ton of data, and rental estimates are one of them. Zillow has rental estimates, particularly for single-family homes.

Another way to get updated rental estimate information is to call up a local property manager to check on rents.

Managing Leads – If you're still stuck on Post-It notes or using a notepad to jot down your leads, you're back in old school days. But if you want to grow your Business and use technology to keep on top of the prospects, then a CRM can fill the bill.

Direct Mail – If your marketing strategy includes direct mail, this is another way to use a list provided by ListSource and upload a mailing service list.

A schedule can be developed to deliver in advance and are in line with your budget and goals. It gives you the chance to prod your targets regularly until they respond.

Improve Tenant Relationships and Asset Management– Real estate investors can control online apartment management software, making it possible for tenants to lease an apartment online, make deposits, pay rent and fees, and submit maintenance requests all on one website.

Using technology enhances the experience of the tenants by making everything related to the property smooth and quick.

Real estate investors have found it possible to monitor their assets and everything going on across their portfolios. They can keep track of expenses, working being done, or organizing property data.

Real estate rental technology is growing. Suppose you're a real estate investor who perhaps owns one or two rental properties and still working your day job, or you're an investor who has been expanding your real estate business and has multiple rental properties. In that case, all of these properties need managing and maintaining at the highest level.

Hiring a property management company is probably the wisest way to go if you cannot manage your properties in the manner they need to be monitored. Its component of ownership is vital.

Owning rental properties is one element of having a real estate business. The other factor is the tenants who are residing in those properties. The income generated by tenants paying their rent keeps those properties solvent and running and keeping your tenants happy where they live.

How your assets are managed directly aligns with their value. As the owner and landlord, you are responsible for having the properties maintained properly, and according to laws instituted by the State, city, and municipality, the properties are located.

Property management is the most important component of your investing undertakings. To serve landlords with ways to manage their properties that make it easier than ever before, several apps, startups, and platforms are cropping up to help this process.

Another reason to hire a property management company is to stay on top of the real estate industry's latest trends. They remain informed about the possible impact that economic trends can have on their business.

Staying prepared about what issues can come to pass over time, they can adapt themselves to any adverse circumstances and keep their clients' best interests in mind while they work to protect their client's investments.

The Developing Property Management Terrain

Having your properties cared for by a property management company can assist you in growing your business. If You are considering doing so, and this is a good time to research some property management firms and interview them. Once you choose one or two, discuss your needs and the rental properties that you own.

The property management company will give you their background and experience in managing properties and the kinds they service. They will also keep you informed about what trends are possibly facing investors and owners.

They recognize the significance of professional relationships

Successful property management firms in the real estate industry are advancing those relationships to endure any financial tempests can menacing the industry as a whole.

They are up-to-date on the current trends

As an investor and landlord, you need to be in the know as well. You can be kept aware of the latest information by researching and reading relevant trade journals and your local newspaper's business part.

As an example, the trend of increased evictions within urban areas that has been a continuing problem for landlords is one that could affect your rental property.

They will make a list of future potentials

It is not about envisioning the future but getting ahead of your need's investor. They are envisioning adjustments in the area where   your   properties   are   located.   To be proactive, make your notes about any changes you are aware of the atmosphere regarding rentals, and perform your research in conjunction with them.

Recognize that there are numerous ways you, as a real estate investor, can have a beneficial relationship with a property management company, and the important information they can provide can help your business grow and maintain its profitability.

The Necessity for Technology

To increase your rental property's value is by offering technology that other property managers or landlords do not. Consider that today's consumers look for options and advantages that add value to a property, particularly when looking for a rental.

If you can satisfy a need and add value for your tenants, they may forgive any possible shortcomings that may happen in other areas.

Although technology can be expensive and your budget may not allow for everything on the following list, just by adding one may give you the ability to lessen any problems with your tenants.

In adding the technology, a yet to come increase in rent can be justified by the addition.

You can install the following to enhance the rentability of your property:

- Online tenant portal

- Home security system

- Smart home technology

- Wi-Fi service

Regardless of the significance and need for technology, keep in mind that most tenants would be ecstatic if there were a dishwasher to use. Being a property manager or landlord is a difficult enough job. It's important to focus on the basics first and not allow the technology to make it all more complex.

Current Technologies Transforming Rental Property Management

Welcome to the world of Cloud-based property management software for the modern manager:

AppFolio

The largest company on this list, this SaaS property management service targeting mid-range to large property managers, was launched in 2007.

Klaus Schauser, a former Entrepreneur of the Year, founded AppFolio raised $30 million from private investors before going public in 2015 at $74.4 million. It indicates that the market has favorably responded to their service.

Pros – AppFolio lets you roam across the range of property management, including tenant screening, accounting, or rent collection.

Cons – Not a good fit for a startup real estate investor, but great for larger property managers.

Buildium

Launched in 2004, this Boston-based company has become embedded in big market share from conventional property managers, gaining 12,500 in 2016 by expanding t0 46 countries worldwide and 1 million residential units. Buildium has many of the same features as AppFolio – accounting for renting collection to tenant screening.

Pros – This is a high-end answer that fits an investor with a couple of properties, making room for future real estate tycoons.

Cons – It does fit the smaller investor, but it's still an expense that can be circumvented with 'do it yourself' tech solutions. Or, you can use the following options.

Cozy

It was the newest technology having launched in 2012. Looking to fill a gap in the property management software marketplace, independent landlords and small property management companies are the businesses Cozy targets.

Pros - The company is designed to fill the void unmet by both AppFolio and Buildium. Cozy truly provides a greater answer for beginning investors and smaller landlords. It's designed to furnish the smaller investor with all the functionalities that the other two companies provide.

Cons – It has a payment option not enjoyed by everyone. However, a small investor's fee is far less than the 10% to a property manager.

Visit all websites to get the latest information on pricing.

Digital Files

More and more paper files and documents are becoming a thing of the past. It's more important today that you go digital.

Paper copies of rent checks, leases, and vendor transactions can be lost. Creating a digital copy of all income, expenses, and all transactions in your business, the worry about losing any paper copy or pages will be a thing of the past. All of it will be on the digital record.

The organization is key to keeping good business records, and keeping digital files makes it easier to do. You can sort all your documents when tax season hits.

You can create varied folders for rental payments, expense transactions, and receipts for all of your rental properties.

Tech-enabled property management is one of the largest breakthroughs for the rental property industry.

About the Author

Neal Hooper is an entrepreneur, investor and the author of bundle "Investing in Real Estate".

A leading authority figure in the world of business, money, finance, and wealth management. He graduated with honors in computer engineering and economics and lives with his wife Kristen in Los Angeles, CA.

Real estate has made him more money than he could ever have imagined, and now, he wants to give back to society. He has decided to put his experiences on paper and started writing books so that everyone gets an opportunity to benefit from his success.

Through his training and coaching programs, he has worked directly with thousands of aspiring investors to jumpstart their rental property journey.

Previously, Neal worked in several corporate real estate and finance roles at large private companies, including at a private equity investment firm covering a wide range of commercial real estate acquisitions.

He will guide you on your journey to financial freedom and early retirement.